Made in the USA
Monee, IL
31 August 2021

76996895R00063